How The Moose Got To Be

Patricia Goodrich

Copyright © 2012 Patricia Goodrich
Cover painting by Patricia Goodrich

VIRTUAL ARTISTS COLLECTIVE
http://vacpoetry.org
ISBN: 978-0-9830091-8-4

Acknowledgment is made for poems published in Bucks County Poet Laureate Anthology, Freshet, Literatura Romania, Mad Poets Review, Texas Poetry Calendar, Two Southwests, and US 1: Journal of Princeton.

Some of these poems were written during residencies and symposiums of the Creative Women: Art and Development Conference, Assilah, and Moussem Feminin Artisque Culturel International, Morocco, sponsored by the Contemporary Painters of Morocco, and Inter-Art Foundation International Art, Aiud, Romania,. Gratitude is expressed to individuals integral to these organizations: Acharifa Lalla Oum Keltoum Alaoul, Wafae El Houdaybi, and Saida Saada; Stefan Balog, Ioan Hadarig, and Robert Lixandru.

*In memory of my mother Frances Burnick Goodrich
& my grandmother Frances Hafner*

*& for other strong women—mentors and friends,
Helen Papashvily & Jere Knight
Bonnie Leach & Elizabeth Raby*

Contents

Is This   7

Sketchbook
Let Space Surround	11
Talking to Sticks	12
Drink Water	13
Silence Leaks	14
Cobalt Blue	15
After Picasso	16
Playground	18
Maximum Security	19
Tumbleweed,	20
Before Coffee	21
First Cup of Coffee	22
What Bodies Tell	23
Apology	24
Sketchbook	25
It's All Relative	30
Gesture	31
Poem in Which I Name My Mother	32
Abstract	33
Potica	35
There are things of which	36
One Dance	37

Muses on Paintings
Muse On Painting a Rabbit	41
How the Moose Got to Be	42
Broken Crow	43
Woodchuck	44
Bear	45
Pig	46
Doe	47
Fox	48
Golden Buddha	49
Dolphin	50
Turtle	51

Self Portrait Without Mirror

Sit With Me	55
The Company I Keep	56
In Public	58
Brushes	59
The Wall Above Her Desk	60
Too Far Gone	61
Imperfect	63
How Does One Choose	64
As Tulips Die	65
Of Value	68
Blue Suede Shoes	69

Selected Lives

Theatro Marcellus	73
Zouber	74
Vasile	75
Ufa'-Shigiri'	77
What I Carry Home With Me	78
Neutral Ground	79
Guide	80
Our Lady	82
Greeting the Living	83
Visit	84
Off Pine Island	85
Key Lime Bistro	86

Is This

a life, a poem,
a lifetime that wants
to be expanded,

each line a grenade
waiting to explode, waiting
for the courageous one,

the fool, the same
to pull the pin—to set
pen to paper

like so many prayers
lit, carried burning
in the wind, so many birds'

unfolded wings, guided by gods
of currents as west and east
separate and meet again,

each breath exhaled, each
story, hers, her mother's,
her others—how to cup them,

pour them into a paper boat
or book bound for other hands?
Is this a sentence

or a blessing?
Break the promise!
Burn the boat!

Sketchbook

Let Space Surround

In a pebbled corner outside the glass wall
of windows insulating this space, balanced,
attached to each other for support are *chamisa*.
Some would call them weed,
refugees from some high desert wind.

Envision a room of them pedestaled
Nothing to be sold to a collector or kept
for posterity. Seed spread, delicate
beyond issues. In this land of adobe
against blue sky, I take a plastic bag,
go collect debris, save the flaxen stem.

Inside, framed by tan walls,
they're barely noticeable. Today
I will approach the studio again.
Think BIG! a friend says,
but I am a creature of little things,
overlooked, broken.

little, I think, *little*

Talking to Sticks

Arroyo, draw, wash,
dry creek bed
flash flood

Red-sticked bush,
I want you—
a twig or two.

White aspen, one root,
how can I separate you from
your brothers and sisters?

I ask *How?*
knowing full well
I would, if given the chance,

strip your skin,
clip a bare branch,
walk away with you.

Drink Water

If this were a heart transplant, the doctor would say my body's rejecting it. Foreign environment whose names even are foreign *arroyo - chamisa*. Air thinned blue, the sky, my blood, oxygen sucked out of it. All curves--the foothills, the buildings, the walls. The walls can't keep out the sky.

Are my shoulders rounding, my back humped to become landscape? I would be absorbed except the ground is too arid to accept me. I imagine a parched, cracked earth, patterned like the geography on the back of my hands. But to crack, there must first be water.

Drink lots of water, I'm told. Powdered dirt that won't even take the track of bobcat on the arroyo slope. Like herbs hanging upside down, the earth has lost its color--what once was ochre, now nondescript. *Drink water.*

Why does the sky without oxygen grow bluer at this altitude and the earth without water lose its red? My heart pumps; my body bridges earth and sky.

Silence Leaks

Last time I listened to the *don't say that*'s interrupting rhythm leaving the virgin poem flat like a tire run to its rim leaded mug whose tea I dare not drink I abandoned it a sinking ship whose run aground on mother's milk homeland's tide I turn against myself

Sow the seed of dissent watch it grow with slanted eyes cross the swamp alligator deep or delta wide wading in wild rice saw the lady half alive chew tobacco from a can the word I want to end on ran past overdue a debt to collect red sun set over blue horizon's purple bruise

Map divided they'd have us believe independence washed out white come commit join the fight against whatever doesn't matter anymore what is wanted is the clanging of our s-words drone on while buttons press silence across the seas body pieces float in air we don't breathe

Hold your breath finger plug in ears choke yourself hands circle neck thumbs on vocal cords true success passes out games we used to play in groups or pairs jump the wire of Mrs. Gray's knee high fence swing a rope swing on a rope fly over creek don't pass go don't ask why or when or who or how high or low

Didn't we crawl belly down winding our way cross the ground bb guns in brothers' hands didn't we duck under white sheeted lines leave flapping blue jeans hanging by one leg bike up cemetery hill race over green graves we knew better than to look behind side splitting how long since your belly ached

Cobalt Blue

What first draws me to the boxes are their wood and their proportion, 22x22x2", hinged to open flat. I envision collage – Cornell would have loved them, their contents secreted. A couple have the lead lining intact. The outside circular labels are an unexpected bonus: *Radioactive Cobalt - 57*. I can't resist bringing them to my studio.

For two days I live with them, an uneasy collaboration. *Radioactive at box edges* a larger black box warns. *Amersh* and *Dupont-Merck Radiopharmaceutical Cobalt-57*. Placing them on a table, ready for cleaning, I stop and check the Internet. *For gamma cameras, 270 days half life* - the numbers don't reassure. What about the other half?

Then the way one thing leads to another, I read *Cobalt-57, Experiments added to B-12* -and a footnote, a page listing *human experimentation with radioactive materials, 1960's*, referring to a federal government agency.

I try to access it and am not surprised to find it blocked, a note saying it is my computer's failure to link. I know those kinds of links, echoes of another presidency, another time, and I wonder will this attempt plus the Cobalt-57 hits be tracked?

The numbered boxes are gone. Too dangerous, I decide. Cobalt: The blue that kills. Pure, rich, the color that costs so much. The color of my coffee mug. The blue that painters die for.

After Picasso

Who abandons a feather duster in wanton disregard blue head silver ball a frame a woman who outlives herself the head white porcelain disconnected bronze holey pelvic bone who are you encased marrow broken fingertips oh juliet you can reach fingers tingle with phantom pain who are the bodies all in clay fired unfired glazed and plain who would cast the first glass whose breath lasts given shape by heat molten past ardor's cooling captured for eternity who sits under a gray canopy whose mind moves as abalone strings suspend their song as if today were any other who can say enough and look away

What time passes a sparrow seed strewn squirrel in the wings waiting for what will be what storm what brown leaf what company he keeps whatever screen divides always there is another side a coin flipped whatever the cost a penny nickel quarter dime loss of love or friend what friendship does allow odds or even more what enemy disavows the lie eyes feast on what's before the butchered pig the pigeon shot for what for perching on rafter thinking he's out of range what kind of man pulls the trigger what woman stands by side what iridescence in the death what spot of blood the pine boards hide what package wrapped casually in the blotting cloth

Where time's consequence is no coincidence where child digs a hole for dog the road where death tracked him down the ground where earth received where tree shadows Sunday mornings where church empty rows and rows where tomorrow lies in possibility where water surges underground cutting stone where children climb king and queen side by side a mockery where pretend rules upside down somersault salute a stick where stem bends flesh where marks blood rises crumbs in pocket flea on fox where woman watches carcass stripped hop hop there are we

Why choose black when blue lay near who cares picasso andywarhol red mug franklloydwright nameless woman whose face a blind man cannot recognize ewe and lamb limestone white newyorkcity in a globe shadow figures who ride the metro no one looks out the window or meets another's eye how hard it is not to care blur the edges what focus it takes no matter where who can move beyond the frame who moves beyond the frame different questions entirely who thinks too much cannot answers find one is not enough two too restricts makes choice inevitable who looks for answers is the fool those who shape the questions rule

Playground

An uneven world we knew it from the first thump of the teeter totter first shove bailing out of a swing too high upside down on monkey bars the only place girls were allowed to be on top boys underneath

Isn't he the skinny one shinnier of trees hands scraped black and blue knees didn't he pay a price was he ever nice

Slide line snakes wait your turn no cutting in once up don't back down even afraid what good's a rule if no one breaks skip the ladder up the slippery way watch out for sunny days shadows cast you can't escape

Maximum Security

Above, a gray dove nestles safely behind bars that cross
a second-story window pane. She is plump and her nest bulges
with bits of sticks and colored string, one broken
egg shell wedged in a corner.

The black bars hold her home in place, and lace curtains behind
assure her privacy even from my grounded point of view.
Still, she could be a statue. If it weren't for her glass marble eyes, she
might not have been seen.

Perhaps when she is done brooding, she will perch here below
where I am, gathered with artists for the formal unveiling
of pedestaled pieces, each carved and polished work
accompanied by sculptors

dressed in their own clothes rather than prison garb—
one of the artists, a tapestry of tattoos himself.
In this maximum security prison with its notorious past,
dignitaries praise the sculptors' works

as blue uniformed guards stand alert, weapons lowered
in a courtyard with red roses, an Orthodox church, not one cigarette
butt littering. One building over, as if part of a lightning rod,
the dove's mate poses,

not cooing or calling his distress, watchful of the pageantry,
secure with sky in sight and his mate behind bars.

Tumbleweed,

In the middle of an East Coast back street
my arms surround you, or perhaps you surrender,
stopping as you do outside my sculpture
studio, offering yourself without
resistance, though I admit to scratches
as I angle your six foot spread through
the heavy glass door, envision you a gilded sun
rising above the *Home-on-the-Range* I've
created here—shotgun shells flying in
vee formation and spouting out of holey basins;
frying pan winged by .22's and .38's,
and (don't be jealous) the portrait of
a man whose heart I glocked repeatedly,
but that was before you came in sight.
To some you are an outlaw; to me,
desired flame. Come, hang here,
my Jesse James.

Before Coffee

From the cusp of morning to the fringe of day I hold on to every waking moment and those which threaten to slip away on far side of blinkless eyes stars darkening alternative universe clipped toenails shed hair lost strands of DNA chromosomes helixing indiscriminately like Cambodian borders under Orange drenched trees

Take a shower light a match see what goes up in flame sift through ash of yesterday searching for tomorrow what I mean to say is where's her clothes what air sucked them off who made us vacuum cleaner of the world did her dolly plug the hole

Whole or holy in whose name does crime erase the course of kings or presidents self-appointed generals not a subject for a sunny day let sleeping dogs lie haven't they

Somewhere the sun is rising be sure of it raise that on your flag flap and flutter in the wind each moment is both beginning and an end take your choice or two or three swing high or low back and forth brush your feet when you enter another's house look both ways before you cross the street or don't skip hop spin jump run retreat

First Cup of Coffee

I know better than to rub my eyes wrinkled craters puffing smoke streaming tears seeing morning sun through veils my mother used to wear sitting on a '49 Ford coupe legs crossed beauty is as beauty does a frog the greatest hopper if you ever caught one or even tried it isn't easy holding on to the slimy side

Letting go is no laughing matter either ask an earthworm as he tries to hole while fingers pinch and pull and he/she doesn't want to let go her holy ground and end up half instead of whole which fault is that who's to blame and does it matter one end or the other wild or tame

Wasn't it just a game a tug of war sanctioned in the name of trout or was it bass we were about the odds were one to one until we graduated to a group numbered off and pulled a rope a rope that burns gung ho hands better a cotton clothesline string 'em up tie 'em to a tree all the possibilities

Opposite directions close to opposition a thumb and forefinger the one that pulls the trigger (keep the thumb low crossed over not linked what goes forward barrels back) pinch the trigger slow and steady a jerk throws off the line of sight flashlight beam tin coffee can count the holes gingerly jagged edge inside smooth rim out

What Bodies Tell

In the face of contradiction does it do to turn the other cheek —a jaguar spotted runs the clock breakneck speed or does it meter how to measure the pleasure of unbroken stride how to recall the feeling of freedom outside after streetlamps light the night the burning leaves ashes in the gutter the sputter of the hose turned off at summer's socket

Underhanded the dealer plays solitaire cheats herself as aces take their places and deuces trail the track of strangers down alleyways of gravel lightning bugged escape from bedside jars the children don't mind morning's deaths a price levied one dark debt they needn't play

Elbows knees wasted waist all are in between ankle wrist neck nearer extremities sex determines places fireflies perch bush and tree a skunk walks across the lawn my eyes follow the white stripe past where I can see does it matter if I act as what's past is present a woman who worries the future into being has no need to look behind to invent untruths no less lies lies the fawn in the night somewhere near the power pole yellow light how does she see she cannot hide and still be found what wild instinct dictates safe is sorry rise rear legs first front knees bent

Left behind footless rabbit lop-sided hop is still a hop though the circle arcs smaller tighter trap tethered by a gyroscope a compass needless north is north no matter the sun has set those who're lost won't find their way the east west cross what's up is also down what's flat is round no map exists for this terrain why do I believe it matters if each journey begins and ends the same

Apology

Cat in a tower rides a rope a tale of daring comedy the fiery fray that weights below the crowds necks cranked and somewhere in her head vertigo plays where'd she go was she there at all are these imaginings of a woman who wishes to trade her places she'd rather be or never gone hold hands or feet or paws retracting claws not required on brick walls or in greeting not entirely rebuked when outstretched hand was refused religion reasons he said with pride briefly I repented my impudence and apologized can you imagine the i'm sorries I've said said repeatedly a habit still in the breaking like chain smoking in a public place disgrace you know the face you turn away in shame i'm sorry mouthed automatically like a vending machine empty quarters jangling no change nickels in a slot where nothing lines up lights blink sirens howl as if the gumballs strewing floor were the copper penny's fault you know the one the dirty cent you picked up in the parking lot tail up luck passing by whatever kind you reach for it

Sketchbook

I.

Perforate Arches cold pressed surface.
The blind lead the sighted.
Nine days I've favored my left leg.

What good is right when someone's left?
Count the grains, and begin again.
My ears fill; blood pressure rises.

Rocky can't stand. These days he lies
by the fire. John rocks by his side.
I don't catch turtles anymore.

For the most part, I leave bones where they lie.
Decide. There is no pain, just haunches
that can't bear weight.

II

Porcelain figurine draped in olive green,
matching bonnet trimmed in white.
The rim distorts.

Acoma pot, all angles, all points.
A straight line is still straight
even if it follows a curve.

Rocks arched by the sea, north of Horseshoe Bay.
An oval O'Keefe would paint through.
Come, walk the pink sand.

Distemper of these days.
Down and up, follow the sun.
Burn, receding hairline.

My hand holds
a flat compass in a round world.
What shades a tree?

Take my leg away, I hop
seven times the brown spider.
Which pearl came from that clam?

Why pry when you can steam?
Wait until tomorrow
tomorrow tomorrow

III

Clay sheep, wooden shepherd.
Chimney rock, Cochiti born.
Make room for me.

Venetian plaster, layer by layer.
Scrape, scratch, sand.
Accept mistakes.

Before the storm I feel it—
the bottoming of barometer.
Grievous body, less relevant than

a sign posted on a public restroom,
Closed for Cleaning,
and the orange cone blocking the door.

You don't know me.
Does blue matter? Is it matter?
I wait for green.

IV

Thick, quilted, cumbersome,
the labels we apply.
Nothing everything, sweet inbetween.

The sky is falling.
Well, only a branch.
I refuse to leave this house.

Milk bottle caps strung by fifth graders
in Cooley School, Cadillac.
Miss Peterson was fat.

I'd move my car, but it means
going out, and I have nowhere else
for it to go.

V

Now is not the time.
There is a reason for burying.
The moon a shallow disc at dawn.
Oak leaves stubborn as sky.
Now is not the time.

Burying the squirrel was not a plan.
Blue sedan trailing close behind.
A finger ringless, diamond without a setting.
Magnolias bud in the fall. I notice them in February.
Songbirds stand and sing. Geese and hawks cry in flight.

VI

To believe you must care. Or
maybe doubt. Blue head, white table.
An address book with names of the dead.

Glasses balanced on the edge of nose
The kind of day when
trees strain to stand upright.

Empire State, SAKS, St. Patrick's
secure in a glass globe.
Sinatra sings *New York*.

What is the difference
between decision and choice?
Black fuzzy slippers with double pompoms.

Clouds thicken yellow.
Yes, there is a sun.
Below, the pawn is moved.

She lies down,
draped in an aqua shower curtain.
Green is a memory.

I cannot move.
The black Hilton pen runs out of ink

VII

Like an accessory

In a room of uncovered heads

One blue scarf knotted.

Will the car flip?

Ants move in a straight line

with lots of turns

The people want it now

My friend has a rule

Do not begin

It's All Relative

I don't believe there must be absolutes a safety thumbed cross your fingers hedge your bets if life's a track run cross country feel the ground stoop for dropped pennies take the long way round

A fugue repeats itself not quite twice the same I can't play or live that way secure in repetition blink an eye fluorescent flicker steady as she goes not my motto disregard man's desire one who doesn't like furniture rearranged sits unmoved through season's change

Autumn's melancholy stop thinking of what to write next cut off trucks rumble from a highway half mile away no insulation from those leaves you can't take it with you so what do you care for what is left behind or is it who that's the rub to grill the stakes so high

Gesture

Words do not a poem make nor take away the silence that resides inside a hollow coconut or a pumpkin waiting for the hallowed scene of moonlight vines creeping a field where turkeys have nothing in common except the shape of bodies and perhaps Thanksgiving

Who's giving thanks these days and for whatever reason the question may arise count on my gratitude rolling down an aisle like a bottle cap loosened rattling like death crept its way up grandma's throat nothing would hold it back though there poems were left unsaid

Much can be made of silence pockets of regret a grudge worn out but mittened still reverie or adoration what love expresses itself but through a distant steady look I feel its caress across a concrete patio how hard not to look back smiling

Poem in Which I Name My Mother

Once a year my mother sends me a loaf.
She, the only daughter who learned
to bake potiça close to the way
her mother made the fine nut bread.
Rightful, the legacy passed to her, Frances,
eldest of three sisters, the one who quit school
in eighth grade and cleaned houses,
so Mary Ann and Sylvia could graduate.

Each year I unwrap the layers of
cellophane and tinfoil that preserve
the loaf on its thousand-mile journey
and offer thin slices to my son and daughter.
I say, *Here's Grandma's potiça*, meaning
my grandma, Frances Hafner, dead thirty-three
years. They assume I mean my mother, older
now than Grandma lived to be, a fact

I can almost ignore through time and miles
that separate. Months ago my mother mailed me
a written recipe, knowing I did not have
enough faith in myself to rely on pinches,
dashes, and feeling. Still I have not tried
to follow it. I am her only daughter. Each
sister had but one, and I am the eldest.
Mother is seventy-one. It is time for me

to learn the recipe, but it takes more
than ingredients and the order of things
listed on a piece of paper. It is
the stirring and resting, the feel of dough
stretched thin as mottled skin, the drape
of a damp cloth against drafts, the evenness
of heat circulating, and always, the timing
when a finger flicks and the loaf rings hollow.

Abstract

Futile

to force the words dissect feelings hoping for a better day or line right now I'd settle for a single syllable but how could alliteration come in to play wind fierce whistle brave pretense stripped naked what else is left except firewood from the fallen or felled is there a difference does it burn the same does it matter to the heated what kind debate but add the wind to the flame sparks fly tinder is the rotting heart once sap is gone and the fallen just look how mighty they've become riding the breeze that once ripped them from the tree now they scamper underfoot and rise to the occasion taunting the solid oak the ragged hickory

Hope

the worn cloth of yesterdays seldom thought of in our better days as if extraneous the fallen feather of a bird not noted by the bird herself picked up by a passerby or at least the impulse there beaten back for fear of avian flu or something worse it is in the worse hope flies near it is the reach not the grasp that gives it lift that tenders flight is it hope drives the mother to push her young out of nest you know they all do not survive the fall wings are broken along the way just when we need reassurance most and find it missing there hope comes with no return without a guarantee yet hope comes and reaches far beyond humanity to where my daughter's black retriever scratches her empty bedroom door

Cheer

contagious goodwill the bearer brings smile appears on lips taste the zest of lemon once sour and you ask why no need for words when cheer abounds see how the world's alight when Eva Mazzucco's near

Miracle

looks us eye to eye wears the face of everyday though there are those who look away or down at shuffling feet unaware that that is where a miracle most oft occurs in the mud of ordinary a puddle of occasional reflection when sun comes out and our faces flower in its rays I looked up through the rain saw a rainbow complete in its dimension arc from mountains to gypsy village splendorous but the miracle complete that came and stayed past expectation was the other bow arced above its twin they stayed long enough for any passerby to stop and stare believing even briefly there is a god somewhere

Forgive

not my strength I write about another's standing next to a brown faced angel chair she's made in memory forgive she says it's God's grace we pass on a white satin robe draped thin ribbons attached by golden baby safety pins to names of three children living and two strands for one *sunrise* and *sunset* with dates just days apart *My Angel* she says too precious too sentimental some will claim yet how many lose a child forgive the one who took her away how many live in a homeless shelter thirty days left for remaining children to stay how many pray

Potiça

Currants crimped as grandma's fingers
sprinkling them over butter-brushed dough.
Like the priest blessing with holy water,
her last rites in our cramped back bedroom.

That flicking wrist, the backs of hands, grandma's
mottled as the raisins and pungent cinnamon
waiting to be hand-rolled into the golden bed.
Then lifted, open ends connected into a ring.
Yeast leavened, rising warm and smooth.
Sweet Jesus. Sweet Bread.

There are things of which

I cannot write.
I don't want to be the new chalk
across a blackboard or the toe nail clipper

of a dog, one that trims too near.
There are travels I cannot translate
except through paint or wooden boxes,

contents pieced together to solve a puzzle
I don't recognize. People who may seem
generic except through portraits gleaned

as we pass each other on cratered roads
or crowded marketplace. Of each
I breathe a memory though I doubt

my presence registered any more
than a bottle of milk on a white shelf,
a plum fallen from a tree, purple

skin split then crushed by a cart
pulled by a red-tasseled horse.
Ah, let the gypsy sing.

Let it not be for nothing
my grandma held me on her lap
and read tea leaves to me.

One Dance

Pouring rivers, forming accidental
lakes, seven continents and a flat diptych Earth,
I've painted the planet. Now I'm through.
Let the pictures dry. It's time for another dimension.

Wood waits. Worm tracked cedar and piñon
lies on the workbench. Pigments from Morocco
mix with egg, gloss polychrome, water.
Figures bend in hues of lapis, paprika, saffron.

The fourth figure, unresolved.
What will color the final direction?
Which way shall she lean? I yearn for emerald,
but Marrakesh's green is too blue.

I need to be sure before I surrender:
Pure titanium white for the mother figure.
I leave each figure's top end unpainted.
Supporting all, an iron ring, carbon black.

Count the rings.
Reflect, as the mirrored base does,
the depth of what we have in common.
One dance, one life.

Muses on Paintings
A Rabbit from a Poem
& other animals living and dead

Muse On Painting a Rabbit

A winter rabbit waits my brush,
but I choose a pallet knife.
I am as frozen as he
might have been, crouched
camouflage against fresh snow
within yards of his windfall hole....
that is not the picture I'll make.
It will be moments after,
after the 12 gauge blast, the beagle's
snouting of the fur. The hand that holds
it upside down, cropped out of sight;
its left leg hacked, leaving
a bloody loose joint, limp body,
ears almost supported by
the picture's perimeter.
Yet, all the while I work
I question *Is this right?*
Neither death nor what I make of it
is so precise. Perhaps the death
I chose for it, too small.
Must I allow the brown jacket
under the neon orange vest, acknowledge
the hand itself? Is this the error,
and is Venetian plaster
not the medium to capture it?
Is this death too smooth?
To give full due, must it be messy and large,
splattered across raw canvas? Or am I
not so wrong except in the naming?
Is this white on white,
severed limb, crimson smear
not of death, but of life,
of what's left dear?

How The Moose Got To Be

Purple is beyond me.
Green, I understand, the necessity
for camouflage, though this painterly
effect is more splotched, poured
as it was before the purple fully dried.
As for cream corn antlers—
or are they horns?—those racks
could hold half-a-dozen tan canvas coats.
They'd never drag, touch the ground.
These stilted legs, like clothesline poles,
knees knocked just enough above hoofed feet
would make even the most serious trophy
hunter break his action into grin and
wallow in the absurdity of puberty.
How much we have in common, the glory
of a crown near ridiculous if you want
to browse around, a lock in love
for which there is no key.
From head to hoof what matters most,
heart's center of gravity.

Broken Crow

Blinded by circumstance,
you've lost the faith
to fly. Yet blind faith is
what is wanted
in these times of trial.
With broken wings did not
prayer do? And who
but God would give
such shimmer to crippled
wings? Luminescent
angel, both the vessel
and the prayer,
your cloak speaks
royalty. Here I find
myself, eyes closed,
writing blind.

Woodchuck

Rather indistinguishable in your flattened state
yet unquestionably dead, the white belly
necessitates paws outlined in black.

Their grace is almost lost—saved perhaps
by the guardian tips of hair, erecting
a spiked halo around your helmet body.

But this is no warrior death, this laying
in state on vivid ground of sunset red,
your earthly body, a map to trace,

a maze of paths to take. What if beaver
or porcupine comes to mind? Are we not
all related in some remove?

Rejoice in the symmetry of shape
that holds the musing muddle of each
inside. Muscles flex, blood pulses, cells grow

and die—chemistry, electricity, H_2O. Held together,
attracted beyond reason. Elemental, this wild love
to hold on. But what of grace?

Does it come only in the letting go?

Bear

The penis is the thing.
Do not mistake
the blood for the bear.
It is the weeping
of a young girl
who isn't there—one
who sat on the edge
of a back bedroom bed,
not knowing how to say no
to the grizzled stranger
while her father lay
drunk, head on the kitchen
table a room away.
What or who led her mother
to leave her job waiting
tables early and
come before blood
to her side?
This is not a memory,
nor is it a dream.
It is a story
told to a daughter
forty years late.
How much it might
have explained.

Pig

Born of a butchering in Romania, you were
the first, taking the place on smooth plaster
of a pretty landscape I'd planned to paint.

Your gutted body became its own delta,
rivers, tributaries. A landscape of its own.
Somewhere you became my father.

A cocky hat he never wore took shape.
It covered him. His death
I hadn't fully mourned until I painted

this rage, the ochre black mustard
red hoofed you, the body bled.

Doe

The leaves I pressed etch the ground
your swollen body floats above.

The arc of neck broken, upside down,
the tongue loosed from the unhinged mouth,

awkward both, uncomfortable in their depiction
yet saved from asphalt's stinking way-

side where I saw you that autumn day,
still see you now. Some things don't change,

no matter how we try to overcome our history.
Evil triumphs as oft as good.

Death, a sure bet. What road we take
to get there is where the question lies.

And to what end is this life? I plant you
in green memory. This is how we survive.

Fox

Orange and white body curled into a ball,
a white-tipped tail masks all except
yellow eyes that track me everywhere
and reflect nights of trotted fence lines,
pee on stray straw and stick, marking *Mine!*
Furtive or sly—words not worthy
of you. The pose, a copy of a painting
I gave my brother Mike, who was most
at home with creatures in the quiet woods.
How like he was, covering his grin, hiding
teeth blackened by a childhood fall.
Maybe what I am doing here,
pouring out these lines and pools,
is laying claim to you from death.
Didn't you leave prints across my brother's grave,
stand boldly roadside in broad daylight?
Didn't you follow me home?
Don't you stand guardian nights
at the foot of my drive
in a circle of light?

Golden Buddha

You plump the bottom
right corner of canvas
while your tail rises,
winding above like a Mingo pine
on a cliff or a branch
of cherry blossoms,
falling petals tracing a path
heavenward. Yes,
you were wise and shining
with pride. Your down-
fall is your story;
the shame
of your demise is mine.
I've reinvented you,
covered you in gilt to mask
my own. And if the blue back-
ground is common, not royal
nor religious, not the blue
that keeps an evil eye away,
but a more pedestrian
blue of kitchen linoleum,
there is no disrespect
intended. After all
that is where
I first knew you,
black beads
staring up at me.
See, your eyes
I've left unchanged.

Dolphin

The jaw I've opened wide. Somewhere
in my attic your bleached skull and vertebrae.
But here in this painting I prefer
to find you awash in white-capped, cotton candy blue.
Some would say your sea should be glass smooth,
but I know you—the way you like
to splash and play.
See the smile I've given back.
Burnished silver bones,
upright posture, proud
of being the center of attention,
you remain a shining beacon, signaling
true beauty lies deep beyond the flesh,
purely happy without a nod toward death.

Turtle

You borne the world on your back, and so you appear,
a cartographer's paperweight, heavy enough to hold
both earth and ocean, flipper feet useless out of water
except for digging holes to bury eggs.
Yet you persist.

I believe in you, in your innate goodness, your lowly
majesty unmoved by politicians' who would divide
beyond the thirteen plates, who would shatter symmetry
in the name of geologic economy..

Near Captiva one fishless day, a great Green rose
as if she were winged and waved to me
before sinking back to sea.
Yes.

Self Portrait Without Mirror

Sit With Me

                    Issa, you are welcome
in my home. I know you will appreciate
I've left cobwebs in the corner of the skylight
and will take no issue with its inhabitants.
You will understand why I keep the jonquils
and daffodils after their yellow shrivels, tinged
by brown. You will not blame me for not changing
the water, nor for the odd rubber band on the lilac
stack of poems haphazardly piled on the floor.

                         Sit with me
for a third cup of coffee—or tea,
which I imagine is what you prefer,
Issa. Let the dangling translucent shells
drown out the dishwasher churning.
Gaze at the gray day.
Write three lines to my ten.
Speak, only if you wish.

                      It is spring, after all.
Though time may shift and pass
through another's hourglass,
I am a woman of dust, not sand,
Watch with me

the buds
unfold imperceptibly
into leaf.

The Company I Keep

Standing Nude
Sitting nude
White plaster
classical nude

Reclining Conte nude
back view
Reclining nude
frontal graphite

Woman dressing
Woman undressed
in front of blue mirror
Self-portrait of someone else

Gravid Mexican Mary
 maybe it was Mary, come down
 to take the human shape,
 yet four-fingered, four toed,

 whose mistake?
 Mary, taken into heaven,
 Mary, God!
Three Marys in one!

Woman with guitar
Joy, brown ceramic naked
on green kitchen chair
Renaissance woman veiled

Woman bearing rock
Corn woman
Blue woman
Inuit mother without hands

Body imperfect
black river stone

In Public

Her breasts droop,
legs spread, fore-
arms rest casually
on thighs.
Seated on a stool,
hair pulled into a bun,
posture without slump,

the shadow she casts
in the living room corner
is that of her back
and of the pedestal
on which she sits.
She doesn't face me.
In fact, she has no face.

Smooth plaster,
still as dust,
she is a blank,
an any woman.
If she were not so
comfortable in her body,
she could be me.

Brushes

She buys her brushes in Marrakesh,
soft bristles of camel hair,
plumed as a peony in bloom.
The pigments come from the same stall
in the souk, ground lapis lazuli, mineral green,
arsenic orange--passions and poisons,
risks the painter is willing to take.
In lidded containers that once held red
Russian caviar, they wait.
Sometimes she reaches for a brush,
strokes its fullness over her cheek
lest a single hair looses its way,
uninvited onto the canvas.

The Wall Above Her Desk

18 inches by 36—the largest space
devoid of art in the entire house
although a shiny picture hanger
hangs there above the window, indicating
the presence of a painting at some time.
She doesn't remember removing it, nor
even what it was.
                      She recalls clearing
the top of the desk, stepping from
the black kitchen stool to the oak surface,
wondering if it would hold her,
estimating measurements and hammering
the nail. An extra hole beneath attests
that accuracy was not her strength—
but whatever was hung didn't stay, and
today she is not inclined to hang another
                      although stacked paintings
prevent her hall closet door's closing
while others edge from under her
queen size bed and the guest room's twins, too.
More are propped in front of bookshelves,
themselves overflowing willy-nilly.
Sculpture litters every surface.
The mahogany china cupboard
is crowned with a fruit still life.
                      Even the plein air porch
is not immune to the spread of oil,
acrylic, litho, pen & ink, steel, stone, glass;
photography and pottery mix with
poetry; and she lives
here somewhere in the muddle.
                      She has built a museum
around herself, allowing only two women
of her own making: one wood, one stone,
neither with a mouth.

Too Far Gone

Field mouse climbs a drift,
his gray, no camouflage now.

I painted too much this morning,
not time, but paint itself,

then rubbed it too solid, too,
erasing the empty spaces

as I went.
Why can't I listen to myself and stop—

going that bit too far as if
a few more swipes with a towel,

a few more words, would fix it—
make something better

when I know better, to leave
well enough alone...

not so different from when I talk
to my daughter, filling air

with words when silence
would better do.

I've learned to keep
an extra canvas near to brush,

pour, and spatter paint leftover,
but how to purge those extra words,

advice unbidden,
love cloaked criticism?

It is one thing to draw a line,
another, not to cross it.

Imperfect

I've added a set of four imperfect Andy Warhol
Marilyn old-fashion glasses to the Rosenthal
Marilyn coffee mugs, bought on clearance.
                    What is so perfect about four—
Four seasons, four directions, four elements,
four friends reading poems together?
At home it's just Marilyn and me
and any one mug or glass will do. Not because
she is so beautiful, but because she is unsure
of that beauty—or only sure of it.

How Does One Choose
after *One Thousand and One Paintings*

the One painting,
the last one,
not the thousand that came before?

Like the last look
before you went blind—
if you had a choice,
would you fill
it with a particular place,
or would it be a familiar face?

What might you see
in the light of a firefly?
When night becomes
the company you keep,
will you listen for the wing
of a great horned's glide.

The last word from your lips,
traveling on your breath
to someone's ear,
would it be *why* or *wait;*
what would he or she hear?
What if no one is near?

What poem
would you conclude with:
the one you wrote
yesterday
or the one you plan
to write tomorrow?

Where does it end?
The last one—perhaps
not *fin*, but *infinity*.

As Tulips Die

Day One

One dozen long stemmed tulips, ivory
looping over an ovoid crystal vase,
water more than half empty, clear beads of
condensation ringing its neck. How far
gone they are, pale green stems jaundiced
yellow, one bloom already shriveled brown,
closest one bent, kissing a Moroccan
glazed blue charger as if to drink from its
sunlit lip. Tea lights long extinguished, three
red ceramic columns of uneven
height here and there. This is an assortment,
rather than a still life arranged. Little
here reflects an artful eye. Instead, a
hurried life, intent, but unattended.

Day Two

In a vase of a dozen, one tulip
stands out, upright, rising above the rest
whose bent heads spread themselves at his feet,
    though
it is they whose bundled stems support.
Step back to see the symmetry: twelve cream
tulips, water low in a clouded vase,
three burnt candleholders angling front and
rear, one blue Sale' bowl as horizon.
All is whole: this throat of vase, capturing
tears of condensation, this rim of plate
lit by southern light, these red cylinders
crowned by candles whose presence is presumed.
And us? Some specks of dust or particles
of light, what part play we in this still life?

Day Three

No elegance resides in these deaths, no
black stamen or pistil letting go, no
pollen's golden rain, no scent lingering.
In glazed reflection of an ink blue bowl
tired tulips soften into velvet
and wither. Each leans away from the
bouquet. Each becomes more individual
as it dies. The cup parts, each petal arced,
curves in carnivore's tongued invitation
—all but one, puckered leaning out to me,
away from window's light that reason says
would pull like full moon reaches for the sea .
As for the line that marks the shore of death,
do we cross it piece by piece, breath by breath?

Day Four–morning

Chaos reigns– rotting stems sunk in stinking
water, a Medusa's head snaking leaves.
Yellow tongues licking, ivory petals
shrivel, pulling away as if each would
have its own death privately. No candles
burn to commemorate though their ruby
glasses match sconces hung in cathedrals
from Russia to Romania, laid on
graves of Czar and peasant alike. A bowl's
scooped as if it were a pond created
by Rasputin, lapis glaze poisonous
enough to drown a maiden tempted to
seek beyond her own reflection from lotus
rimmed shore to the single naked blossom.

Day Four—evening

I don't want to look at limpid flowers
and what's become of them...nor name them
particularly, though I do admit
twisted leaves, intertwined, their mucus stems
scum bled leanings in rancid water, more--
these misshapen petals each become
individually grotesque heads--that this
untoward crapulence is what I'd choose.
(Glibly said, but not the truth.) Night shrouds panes
black, yet by reflection illuminates
the other side, and still I look for more.
These ordinary deaths...so artfully
arranged in life...dominate. Their blight
no less mine. Death seems clearer in the night.

Day Four—night

As if description could replace meaning
when soft words do most deflect, rain-
drops breaking puddle's surface, distorting
faces, masking what deeper lies beneath.
And so it is: The dying tulips, quite
ugly in their final death, shadow blue's
etched calligraphy while three red pillars
stand static in their line. Perhaps it is
the eking of the deaths, or their over-
lapping nature. Something there is beyond
that troubles me. Yet, what but to words can
I retreat, the curtain that keeps me from
drawing near. I hide behind reflection's
screen, safely absent in this deadly scene.

Of Value
for Laurel

The skull is packed in my attic.
Perhaps I should warn my daughter,
assuming she'll be the one to sort my life once it's done.

The bone doesn't smell anymore. It took a soaking in bleach and
days of airing in the sun, not so much because of the skull itself
but its tough cartilage— protruding.

No one else I know has one.
It may not even be legal, so, too, I should advise her
not to claim it as part of the estate.

Twice I've begun to list art I've collected.
I become distracted somewhere between paintings
and sculptured Papashvily stones.

Books are beyond me. Suffice it to say she should check
for first editions, autographed volumes of poetry.
Don't lose Woody Guthrie's Vol. 1, mimeo union song sheets.

The value of the antler collection may be negligible. But this
dolphin skull and its links of winged vertebrae,
holding on to things like that, my daughter, can save you.

Blue Suede Shoes

Lambertville, N.J.

Better than Carl Perkins.
Even than Elvis Presley.
I covet the shoes the moment I see them.
Smooth, cool blue, fine suede.
Gold buckles for the straps,
Shaped to fit, riding over toes
to meet leather soles so thin
they could belong to slippers
Unsized, custom-made, #16112/414,
LaRay Footwear, New York, 1960.
Shoes not for scuffling along
a city street. They belonged on feet
that measured music on its way
to places we could only follow,
the feet of a duke. A certain elegance.
I want to be the one to preserve it.
The shoes sit on the same glass shelf
as a letter written by Queen Victoria
two days after the death of her husband.
They are number 965 of 990 in the auction catalog.
I wait, unable to believe that there won't be
a lot of someones with a lot more money
to outbid me. But didn't I steal
the life-sized, low-fired raku sculpture of *Joy*,
a brown nude seated on a green kitchen chair,
for a price so low it's embarrassing.
She will be such good company.
And so I bide my time almost nine hours.
Then it is over fast.
The auctioneer, tired or seeing passion
in the quick movement of my paddle,
hammers *Sold*.
No one has had a chance to bid, but me.
I can hardly believe they will be traveling

at my side. The blue suede shoes of Duke Ellington.
Elegance is in the details, thin golden buckles,
fine stitching of smooth skins,
the thread unbroken.
I'll keep them just long enough.
Already I'm searching for the right person
to pass them on to, someone who appreciates
what it is to own one elegant pair of shoes.

Selected Lives

Theatro Marcellus
Rome

One stone is all I desire. Any one will do
to hold onto this brief visit.
Two columns white, lights from below,
the moon above pretending to be full
for lovers walking hand in hand, kissing
near flowing fountains—for only this I cross
the four traffic lanes, six if you count the Vespas
weaving in paths of their own making,
helmeted couples astride these chariots,
grandiose perhaps, but excess excused
by the crumbling arches of Theatro Marcellus
where an audience in its amphitheatre
relives comedy and tragedy while above
an occasional room is lit and like a crown
a turreted miniature castle rises.
Why not be brave? What risk is there, I ask,
except my bus's imminent departure?

But two men, young and old tend the table
which separates those who pay their way
and those who are mere passersby.
The young looks to the old, who in turn
turns away, a smile pulling at his lips.
The younger guides me along the fence
that only now I notice runs the whole length
of grounds, allowing none to stray.
Then in the false full-mooned light
he climbs over to the other side
and retrieves one white limestone, or is it marble?
He places it, soft and smooth as chalk, in my hand
perfect for my palm to cup as fingers polish.
Is this all right? Not his words,
but whatever language he uses
we both understand.

Zouber

Black hair halos his face, his body.
Dark eyes do more than look.
He does not caution me,
but says he feels inside me
a depth, a strength. I thank him.
I, who so often apologize
my way through life
have no need to say more.
Words do not seem
to hold an important place.
He is a Kurd living in Germany.
But his limited English,
my few foreign words
are spliced together—or perhaps
stitched by hands as we try
to find a common language.
His wild scarved head,
my bare face.
Neither of us turns away.

Vasile
Aiud, Romania

Once I saw him dance
without a partner on a crowded patio.
Handsome in a gentlemanly way,
the quiet, dark-haired, dark-eyed
man often eats alone, or seems alone
even seated next to others.
Evenings he stands on the periphery.

Yet, he is not aloof.
More like a gentle phantom
here in a storage warehouse
with cracked amber windows nine of us share—
sculptors and painters from Morocco,
Syria, Serbia, Kosovo, Macedonia, Bosnia-
Herzegovina, Romania, USA—
his quiet presence lights the farthest reaches.

He sweeps clear a space in the rear.
and makes his studio from the rubble—
piles of insulation salvaged from old chairs,
broken windows, sacks from chicken feed.
Two puppies piss underfoot, roll
their low-slung, flea ridden bodies,
bury noses in sawdust. They tip his paint,
steal conductor chips from his collage.
Vasile never raises his voice.

For a week he barely does more than nod.
He seems to speak little English.
Yet when I mention Lithuania,
his face lights. Yes, he has been to Kronos.
He is Moldovan, studied art in Moscow,
was in Afghanistan with the Russian Army.
Now he lives in Bucharest.

After never having seen him
in conversation with anyone here,
I am more surprised when he says
in careful English
What means most to me here is
to talk freely with artists
from other countries...
To know them...
To know their art.

Ufa' – Shigiri'
Sverdlovsk Province, Federation of Russia

Pigs and pets have no place here, yet
that is not to say life is cruel or
there is no room for beauty.
Outside, windows are framed by distinct intricate
carvings on houses painted blue, green,
or salmon, all with white trim.
Inside, women flower their aprons
with embroidered bright stitches,
taking place of summer rampant blossoms
whose blooms fade into late September.

Almost bereft of dogs
or even cats, though those
less noticeable in their absence,
settled nearly a thousand years,
built on the plain along the River Ufa',
fenced by forests of birch and pine,
the Tatar village's wooden houses extend
into barns filled with firewood and hay
that give shelter to sheep and goat and cow
from Siberian winter's cold.

With wolf and bear and winter ever at their doors
taking in more mouths to feed is itself
not a wise deed. Nothing extra
to starve or freeze
when the terrible times come—as they must,
sloughing through the season of thaw's
mud, shuffling on the swaying
wooden bridge suspended across the River Ufa',
uniting the Muslim village until the freeze comes
and all can walk on water.

What I Carry Home With Me

A wooden loom—his mother's,
the imam said, one she used
to weave the family's towels—

The *caw* of iridescent ravens settling
on tips of yellowing birch
surrounding the centuries' graves—

A fist-sized skull of uncertain origin
I dug out of the Ufa' River's bank,
making the mistake of leaving

its lower jaw behind.

Neutral Ground

To write the words, to paint the scene,
to leave us from the outside looking in.
Though there is more unexplained,
I write the bubbling spring here
in scribbled script before I read
the note you sent, how you recall it,
too, as if it were a sacred perking at our feet
as we walked the cart two-track, feeling
our way toward what we never speak.

Nor do I now tell you how our thoughts
have crossed today on waves through air.
I keep the coincidence and don't write back
until time creates its own safe barrier.
But we both had watched the bubbling hole
turn into rivulets that crossed the path
and became a waterfall and carved a stream
that feeds a mountain river that makes its way
to the ocean that both separates and binds us together.

Guide

To the north on a mountainside
light transforms itself into snow;
to the east purple thunderclouds
form a curtain behind Enchanted Rock.
A man whose real name I cannot say but who calls
himself Orlando guides us through Acoma pueblo's
thousand year old village, telling stories of stolen boys
and a three-layered graveyard forty feet deep,
earth basketed up the 357 foot cliff on women's backs.
He speaks quickly, never repeating words, punctuating
with four choreographed gestures and a numerical mantra.
What he says we remember.

Later sitting with the group, I tell him
I'd heard he'd been a teacher. He seems surprised I care.
"Yes, but I was burned and quit."
"Burned out", I say.
"No. Burned."
That is when he says, *Here. Feel.*
He takes my hand to his side
and my fingers, even through his turquoise shirt,
trace skin channeled like eroded pathways.
This story that comes is his own:

A better cook than hunter,
while his father and brother stalked deer,
Orlando stayed behind building the campfire.
A sudden gust of wind raised flames
that encircled and burned him. He was saved
by rolling under a patch of sage into a pocket of earth,
He remembers looking at his watch, then
and later when he came to.
The numbers were sacred: 4:12—7:21.
He dragged himself to his truck and called for help.
Four months in a hospital; a teaching career left behind.

His telling is informative, rather than dramatic,
as if we are his students. There is only the one gesture.
Why am I the one he touches?
I do not pull away.
His left hand guides my left hand,
a direct line heart to heart,
his shirt no insulation for the skin's ridges,
like the folds of the mountain
leading to the sacred mesa.

Our Lady
for artist Leo Jeanette

I bring her home with me, Our Lady of Guadalupe radiant, ringed with maize yellow, standing on an angel's wings, robe cascading in turquoise folds over a clay red gown.

Covered from head to toe, only her face shows, flesh toned lighter than I would expect. How can its two dots and slash create so much feeling?

The cherub's head upon whose wings she stands elevates her. We know she is no longer earthly. Her pure colors and simple lines draw my eyes.

But when I hold her, it is my hands that take her to my breast. It might be the smoothness of the enamel pink. I like to think it is the carver's hands, shaping and sanding, feeling his way.

Greeting the Living

Perhaps the reason I speak my mother's name when the priest asks for other intentions of the Mass is because here at the church in the pueblo of San Ildefonso the dead are not separated off in a fenced corral to be visited on holidays or anniversaries - or not at all. Here the graves of the dead line the walk to the front door. They are the churchyard.

Nor are the graves flat and swept clean like the plaza beyond the low adobe wall. Each grave rises in greeting, its mound marked with a cross of stone reaching from head to toe. Red, blue, yellow plastic flowers pay tribute, too. And so when I walk past them and recall that this time last year I flew home to see my mother for the last time, she stays with me inside the church throughout the Mass.

I recognize Maria Martinez's descendents in the pews; the photographs of her daughter and son-in-law on a striped blanket covering the table with their pottery black bear and candle holder. The vessels holding the Body and Blood of Christ are Native American. The bleeding Crucifix, statues and arches, Hispanic. The congregants are both from the pueblo and outsiders, like me. The collection baskets, far from full.

Though it has been years since you attended Mass, Mother, you would like it here. Before communion, yours is the last name said, *Frances Goodrich*, and it echoes in the adobe, its sound far from where you raised me in Michigan, but reaching you, I pray.

Visit

for Trapp

The night before I leave I dare ask, *Are you lonely?*
Then so nervous, I cut his answer short and never really hear

the reply, but still I feel good and brave and almost a good mother.
I resist telling him how awkward, how in search of words

to make connection, how so often nothing comes,
how I found after my mother's death a newspaper clipping

she kept next to her bed, *How to talk to your children,*
surprised that she, too, might have wanted something more.

But I am here, wanting to be close, sitting next to my son,
grown and gone, a man I see only twice a year, and he says,

"I think it's really neat that you're going to all those places,
doing all those things,"—like he's proud, and I'm surprised.

And when he takes me to the plane, he waits until every stone
is shifted in suitcases and repacked to pass the check-in weight,

and he watches while Security checks me through, satisfied
extra rocks in my carry-on are only rocks and not weapons and

my hollow leg is not a cache and my hands hold no explosive residue.
He stands on the other side of the safety glass window, cradling

my overweight—a bag of dirty laundry and three more stones
I collected while he fished at Clark's Fork the day before

and I was searching for something to say in the inbetween.
How good to know he understands
and they'll all be there for me to claim, come spring.

Off Pine Island
Gulf Coast, Florida

One manatee, three dolphins. I take count
as if the being alone weren't miracle enough.
Such company to keep, their diving and
skimming the surface of this sheltered bay,

and I, trolling for Spanish mackerel, or whatever else
willing to bite, a pole in my right hand, camera in left
until I leave it in the boat's swivel seat to will
these water mammals closer, but not too close
to the propeller nor to the silver spoon riding the wake.

"Let out more line," I'm told. I do and the lure sinks.
I wait for the creature's rising, confident it will come
although from what direction and for how long
I do not know. But this sunshine,
this water, this moment, of these I am sure.

Key Lime Bistro
Captiva Island

This time I am a pound under weight
and a stranger waiting at the same gate
for a flight north to Cleveland
doesn't act as if it is anything but ordinary
when I approach him and his New York Times,
and ask if can I buy the Arts section from him.
He gives it to me, free and clear, and when
I inquire about the eight-inch Churchills
he has sticking out of a bag, he gives me
one of those, too. I say, "Thank you.
I have a friend who will enjoy it."
"It's a good one", he says, and goes back
to someone, perhaps his wife, on the phone.

This time my suitcase is empty
of stone and shell, broken shards
of others' discarded lives.
This time I carry fresh key limes
and the sounds and smells of a bistro,
its blackened grouper and string-plucked
songs of Antonio Carlos Joabim.
We are heading towards overcast skies and
snow and temperatures of twenty degrees.
But ask me what kind of trip I've had.

Patricia Goodrich is a writer and visual artist. Her poetry has been translated into Chinese, Lithuanian and Romanian. Goodrich has received Pennsylvania Fellowships in Poetry/Creative Nonfiction and has been nominated for Pushcart Prizes in poetry and fiction. She is a recipient of fellowships and residencies through the Andy Warhol Foundation, Atlantic Center for the Arts, Europos Parkas (Lithuania), Inter-Art Foundation (Romania), Leeway Foundation, Makole Sculpture Symposium (Slovenia), Puffin Foundation, Santa Fe Art Institute, Vermont Studio Center, and Yaddo. Recent collections of poetry include *Red Mud* and *Verda's House*.

CPSIA information can be obtained at www.ICGtesting.com
Printed in the USA
BVOW011719090912

299929BV00001B/12/P